SECOND EDITION

4 LET'S GO

Workbook

Steve Wilkinson
Karen Frazier
Ritsuko Nakata
Barbara Hoskins

OXFORD
UNIVERSITY PRESS

Let's Talk

A. Read and connect.

Hi! I'm Nina. I'm ten years old. I live in Northwood. I have one sister and one brother.

Hello! I'm Mel. I'm nine years old. I live in Cold Spring. I have one brother.

Hello! I'm Randy. I'm eleven years old. I live in Danville. I don't have any brothers or sisters.

Hi! I'm Cindy. I'm twelve years old. I live in Middleton. I have two sisters.

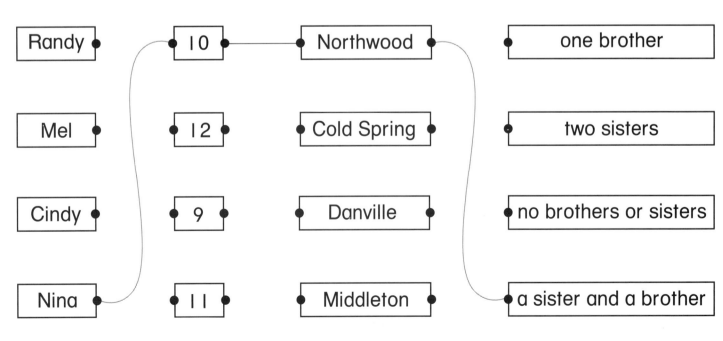

Randy	10	Northwood	one brother
Mel	12	Cold Spring	two sisters
Cindy	9	Danville	no brothers or sisters
Nina	11	Middleton	a sister and a brother

B. Fill in the blanks.

1. This is Nina.

   She's ten years old.

   She lives in _____

   She has _____

2. This is Randy.

   He's _____

   He _____

   He _____

3. This is Cindy.

   She's _____

   She _____

   She _____

4. This is Mel.

   He's _____

   He _____

   He _____

C. Write the answers.

1. What's your name?

   _____

2. How old are you?

   _____

3. Where do you live?

   _____

4. Do you have any brothers or

   sisters?

   _____

A. Make sentences.

small

tall

1. The cat is small.

   The dog is smaller.

2. Joan is tall.

   Ned _____

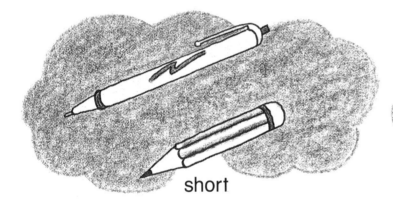

short

young

3. _____

   _____

4. _____

   _____

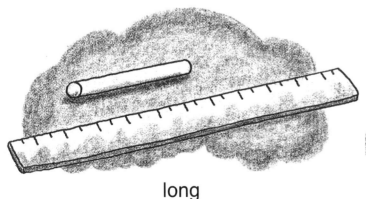

long

big

5. _____

   _____

6. _____

   _____

B. Circle and write the answers.

Peter   Mary

Mike   Jane

1. Who is older?

   Mary is older.

2. Who is taller?

   _____

car   fire truck

thin snake   fat snake

3. Which one is bigger?

   _____

4. Which one is longer?

   _____

C. Write the answers.

Alex   Scott

1. Is Alex older?

   No, he isn't. He's younger.

2. Is Scott taller?

   _____

3. Is Alex shorter?

   _____

4. Is Scott younger?

   _____

Let's Read

A. Read the postcard and answer the questions.

1. Where does Henri live?

_____

2. How old is he?

_____

3. What is his brother's name?

_____

Write your own question and answer.

4. _____

_____

_____

_____

_____

_____

Dear Pen Pal,
My name is Henri. I live in France. I am eight years old. How old are you? I have an older brother. His name is Pierre. He is ten years old. Do you have any brothers or sisters? I have an orange and black cat. Do you have a cat, too?

Your friend,
Henri

B. True or false? Check the answer.

1. Henri lives in France.   ☐ True   ☐ False

2. He has a younger brother.   ☐ True   ☐ False

3. His younger brother is nine years old.   ☐ True   ☐ False

Write your own true or false sentence.

4. _____   ☐ True   ☐ False

_____

C. Write a letter to Henri.

Dear Henri,

My name is _____

_____

_____

_____

_____

Your friend, _____

_____

D. Circle and write.

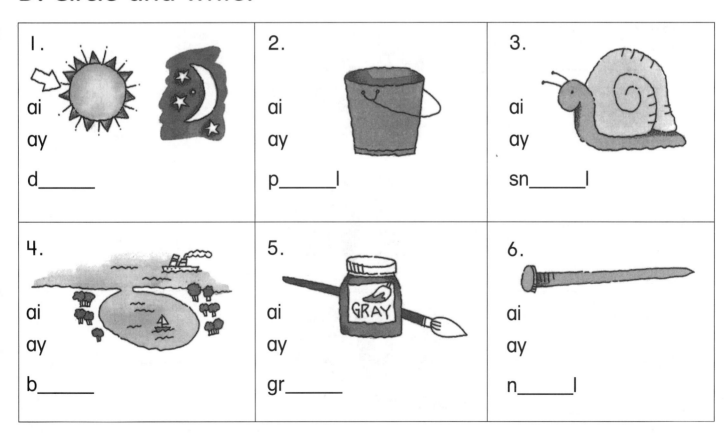

1.
ai
ay
d_____

2.
ai
ay
p_____l

3.
ai
ay
sn_____l

4.
ai
ay
b_____

5.
ai
ay
gr_____

6.
ai
ay
n_____l

Let's Chant

A. Fill in the blanks.

1. He _____ a sister.   2. She _____ a brother.

3. They _____ a brother.   4. They _____ a sister.

B. Fill in the blanks.

1.
I have a brother.

I have a _____, too.

2.
_____

_____
_____ a sister, too.

3.
I have a sister.
I have a _____, too.

I don't have a _____, but I have a _____ , Lou.

Let's Listen

A. Write the answers.

1. Who is taller?

_____

2. Who is shorter?

_____

3. Is Sue younger?

_____

B. Write the questions.

1. _____

The fire truck is bigger.

2. _____

The fire truck is longer.

3. _____

No, it isn't. It's smaller.

C. Unscramble and write.

This is Jason.

1. in Lakewood. He lives

_____

_____

2. eleven old. He years is

_____

3. sister has two He one

brothers. and

_____

Let's Talk

A. Match and connect.

What do you do? •	• I make hamburgers and french fries.
Where do you work? •	• I'm a cook.
What do you usually do? •	• Yes, I do. It's a lot of fun.
Do you like your job? •	• I work in the kitchen.

B. Write the questions and the answers.

firefighter	salesclerk	mail carrier	businessperson

1. What does she do?

   She's a _____

2. _____

   _____

3. _____

   _____

4. _____

   _____

C. Unscramble the words and write the sentences.

1. f r l o t i s = <u>florist</u>

<u>He's a florist.</u>

2. a b k r e = _____

_____

3. r e c s r t a e y = _____

_____

4. f h s m i e r a n = _____

_____

5. a b n k r e l l t e = _____

_____

6. s e d i t t n = _____

_____

Let's Learn

A. Write the words.

1. _____ a clinic _____

2. _____

3. _____

4. _____

5. _____

6. _____

B. Write sentences.

1. A baker works in a bakery.

2. A florist _____

3. A factory worker _____

4. A businessperson _____

5. A bank teller _____

6. A doctor _____

C. Fill in the blanks and do the puzzle.

Across

2. A _____ makes things.

3. A secretary types letters.

5. A _____ catches fish.

7. A _____ fixes teeth.

Down

1. A _____ helps sick people.

4. A _____ bakes bread.

5. A _____ sells flowers.

6. A _____ counts money.

Let's Read

A. Fill in the blanks.

likes
types
uses
uniform
talks
secretary
office

This is Donna Miller. She's a _____. She works in an _____. She doesn't wear a _____. She _____ letters.

She also _____ on the telephone.

Sometimes she _____ the computer.

She _____ her job.

B. Write the answers.

1. What is her name?

_____

2. What does she usually do?

_____

3. Where does she work?

_____

4. Does she wear a uniform?

_____

Write your own question and answer.

5. _____

_____

C. Circle and write.

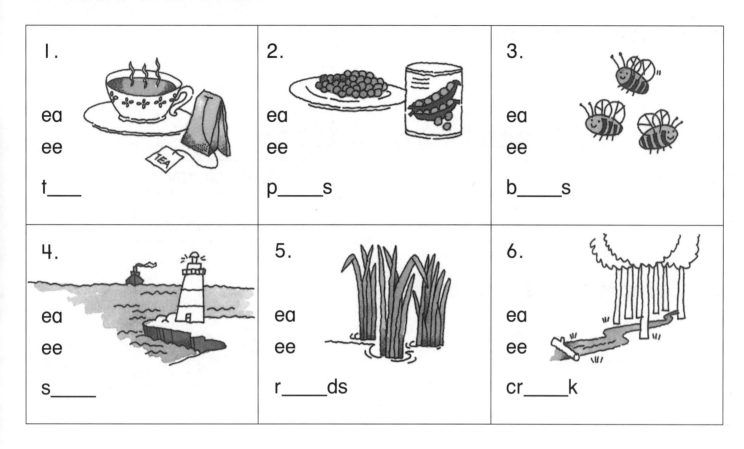

1.
ea
ee
t___

2.
ea
ee
p____s

3.
ea
ee
b____s

4.
ea
ee
s____

5.
ea
ee
r____ds

6.
ea
ee
cr____k

D. Fill in the blanks.

1. She drinks _____

   and eats _____

2. The _____ were

   flying near the _____

3. The frogs were playing in the

   _____ near

   the_____

Let's Sing

A. Match and connect.

1. A dentist ● ● bakes bread all day.

2. A secretary ● ● fixes cars all day.

3. A mechanic ● ● fixes teeth all day.

4. A baker ● ● types letters all day.

B. Complete the sentences.

1. Sid is a factory worker.
   He makes things all day.

2. Nita _____
   _____

3. Nick _____
   _____

4. Jenny _____
   _____

5. Peter _____
   _____

6. Betty _____
   _____

Let's Listen

A. Fill in the blanks.

_____   Andy _____   _____ Lori _____   _____

1. Her name is _____

   She is _____

   She works in an office.

   She types letters.

2. His name is Paul.

   He is a florist.

   He works in _____

   He _____

3. His name is _____

   He is a dentist.

   He works in _____

   He fixes teeth.

4. Her name is Jill.

   She is _____

   She works in a bakery.

   She _____

B. Write the questions.

1. _____

   He's a firefighter.

2. _____

   A doctor helps sick people.

Let's Review

A. Match the questions with the answers.

Where do you live? •   • I'm a teacher.

Do you like your job? •   • I live in Oak Grove.

What do you do? •   • No, but I have two brothers.

Do you have a sister? •   • Yes, I do.

B. Write a question for each answer.

1. _____

I live in Westbury.

2. _____

No, but I have a sister.

3. _____

I'm a bank teller.

4. _____

Yes, I do.

C. Use the words to make sentences.

Jack

Jim

tall   Jack is taller. _____

young   _____

old   _____

short   _____

big   _____

long   _____

short   _____

small   _____

D. Unscramble and write the answers.

1. What does he do?

    is | florist. | He | a

    _____

    Where does he work?

    shop. | He | flower | in | works | a

    _____

2. What does she do?

    doctor. | is | She | a

    _____

    Where does she work?

    a | in | clinic. | works | She

    _____

E. Write the questions or the answers.

1. What does a factory worker do?

    _____

2. What does a fisherman do?

    _____

3. _____

    A secretary types letters.

4. _____

    A bank teller counts money.

Let's Talk

A. Connect the numbers.

six	1	third
two	2	tenth
five	3	fourth
one	4	seventh
seven	5	first
nine	6	eighth
three	7	second
ten	8	sixth
eight	9	fifth
four	10	ninth

B. Write the missing number.

1. _____fourth_____, _____, _____sixth_____

2. _____, _____eighth_____, _____ninth_____

3. _____third_____, _____fourth_____, _____

4. _____eighth_____, _____ninth_____, _____

5. _____first_____, _____, _____third_____

6. _____sixth_____, _____seventh_____, _____

C. Complete the sentences.

1. Jean was <u>third.</u>

2. Brad was _____

3. Tim was _____

4. Jake was _____

5. Nancy was _____

6. Meg was _____

D. Write the answers.

1. Who was first?

_____

_____

2. Were Amy and Ellen second?

_____

_____

3. Was Patty second?

_____

_____

Let's Learn

A. Write the questions and answers.

| playing catch | chasing butterflies | picking up trash |
| skateboarding | roller-skating | playing tag |

1. What was he doing?

   He was _____

2. _____

   _____

3. _____

   _____

4. _____

   _____

5. _____

   _____

6. _____

   _____

B. Answer the questions.

1. Was she feeding the ducks?

   <u>No, she wasn't. She was skateboarding.</u>

2. Was he taking pictures?

   _____

3. Were they roller-skating?

   _____

4. Were they picking up trash?

   _____

C. Answer the questions.

1. What were you doing at 10:00 this morning?

   _____

2. What were you doing at 2:00 yesterday afternoon?

   _____

Let's Read

A. Fill in the blanks. Use the words from the box.

| sang songs |
| fish |
| good |
| camp |
| swimming |
| raining |
| arts and crafts |

Dear Mom and Dad,

I like _____ a lot.

On the first day I was

_____ and I saw

a lot of _____.

Yesterday it was _____.

We did _____

and we _____.

I'm having a _____

time.

Love,

Kathy

B. True or false? Check the answer.

1. Kathy is at camp.   ☐ True   ☐ False

2. She was hiking on the first day.   ☐ True   ☐ False

3. She sang songs and saw a movie.   ☐ True   ☐ False

4. She's having a good time.   ☐ True   ☐ False

Write your own true or false sentence.

5. _____   ☐ True   ☐ False

C. Circle and write.

1. y ie d____	2. y ie fl____	3. y ie t____
4. y ie p____	5. y ie cr____	6. y ie sk____

D. Complete the sentences.

1. The _____ was in

   the _____

2. The _____ is in

   the _____

3. Is the bird _____ ing?

   No, it isn't. It's _____ ing.

Let's Chant

Fill in the blanks.

race	ride	did	play	baseball
won	camp	fun	do	fine
fun	win	swim	pizza	food

1.

How was _____?

It was _____.

We had a _____.

Did you _____?

Yes, we _____.

2.

Did you _____ a horse?

Did you _____ in the sun?

Yes, we _____.

We had _____.

3.

How was the _____?

It was _____.

We had _____ all the time.

4.

What did you _____?

What games did you _____?

We played _____ every day.

Let's Listen

A. Write the answers.

SPORTS DAY
1st Blue Team
2nd Green Team
3rd Red Team
4th Yellow Team
5th Orange Team

1. Which team was first?

   The blue team was first.

2. Which team was third?

   _____

3. Was the yellow team second?

   _____

4. Was the green team fifth?

   _____

B. Write the answers.

1. What was he doing?

   _____

2. What was she doing?

   _____

3. What were they doing?

   _____

4. What was he doing?

   _____

5. Was he chasing butterflies?

   _____

6. Were they skateboarding?

   _____

Let's Talk

A. Write the names of the months.

B. Complete the sentences.

1. January _is the first month._   2. August _____

3. May _____   4. November _____

5. July _____   6. October _____

C. Match and connect.

6/15 = June 15th

10/15	February 17th
2/17	December 20th
9/13	August 24th
12/20	September 13th
8/24	October 15th

D. Write the answers.

1. When's your birthday?

It's on May 8th.

2. When's your birthday?

_____

3. When's your birthday?

_____

E. Answer the questions. Write the dates.

1.

2.

3.

1. When's your birthday?

_____

2. What's the date today?

_____

3. What was the date yesterday?

_____

Let's Learn

A. Fill in the blanks.

1. have → _____
2. go → ___went___
3. fly → _____
4. meet → _____

B. Fill in the blanks and write the names.

_____Mike_____   _____   _____

_____   _____   _____

1. Mike _____ to a soccer game on his birthday.

2. Pete _____ his favorite rock star on his birthday.

3. Dave _____ in a balloon on his birthday.

4. Mary _____ out to eat on her birthday.

5. Jenny _____ bowling on her birthday.

6. Pat _____ a party on her birthday.

C. Write the answers or questions.

1. Did he have a party on his birthday?

2. Did she go bowling on her birthday?

_____

3. _____

Yes, he did.

4. _____

Yes, she did.

D. Write and draw.

What did you do on your birthday?

_____

_____

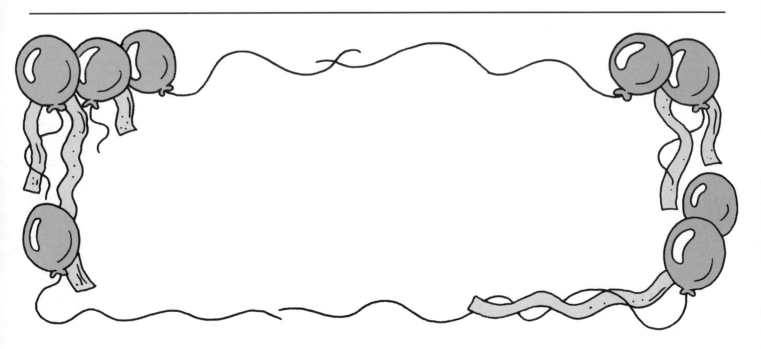

Let's Read

A. Fill in the blanks.

November 4th
eleven
skateboard
went bowling
Diary
birthday
fun

Mike's _____

_____

Today is my _____.

I'm _____ years old.

I got a new _____.

I _____ with my

friends. It was _____.

B. Write in your diary.

_____

_____

_____

_____

_____

_____

_____

C. Circle and write.

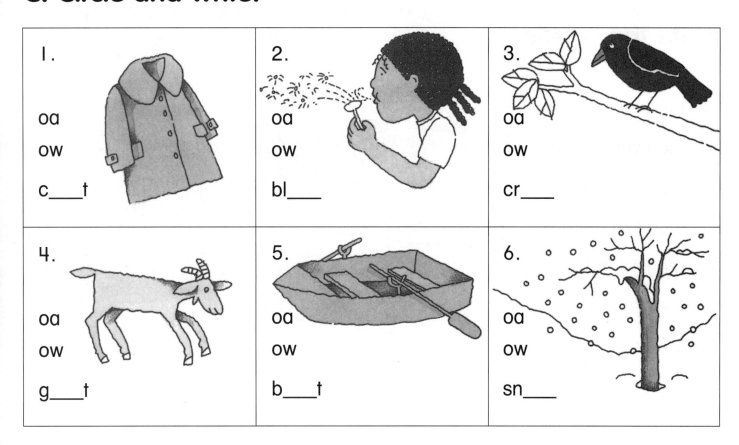

1.
oa
ow
c___t

2.
oa
ow
bl___

3.
oa
ow
cr___

4.
oa
ow
g___t

5.
oa
ow
b___t

6.
oa
ow
sn___

D. Find these words.

boat
goat
coat
blow
crow
snow

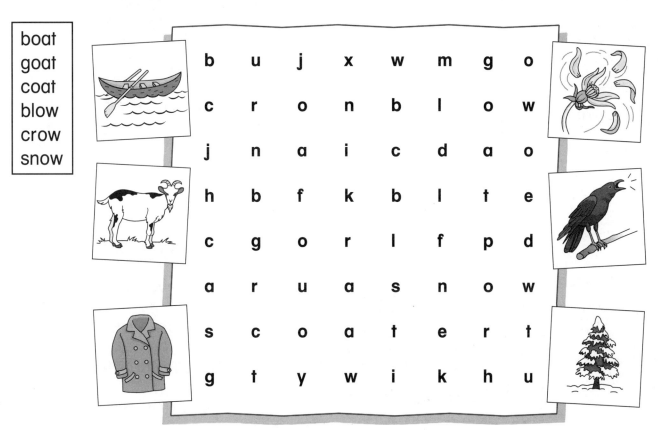

b	u	j	x	w	m	g	o
c	r	o	n	b	l	o	w
j	n	a	i	c	d	a	o
h	b	f	k	b	l	t	e
c	g	o	r	l	f	p	d
a	r	u	a	s	n	o	w
s	c	o	a	t	e	r	t
g	t	y	w	i	k	h	u

Let's Sing

Write the words.

Across

3. the tenth month

5. the twelfth month

7. the ninth month

8. the third month

10. the first month

11. the fifth month

12. the seventh month

³O c t o b e r

Down

1. the sixth month

2. the eleventh month

4. the eighth month

6. the second month

9. the fourth month

A. Write the missing months.

1. ____April____ , ____May____ , _____ , _____

2. ____December____ , _____ , _____ , ____March____

3. _____ , ____September____ , _____ , _____

B. Write the numbers.

____1st____ , _____ , ____3rd____ , _____ ,

_____ , _____ , _____ , _____ ,

_____ , ____10th____ , _____ , _____ ,

_____ , _____ , _____ , _____ ,

_____ , _____ , ____19 th____ , _____ ,

_____ , ____22nd____ , _____ , _____ ,

_____ , _____ , _____ , _____ ,

_____ , ____30th____ , _____ , _____

C. Write the answers.

1. What did he do on his birthday?

_____

2. Did she go horseback riding on her birthday?

_____

Let's Review

A. Write the answers.

Marta   Sid   Nick   Judy   Betsy   Max   Dana   Bud

1. Who was first?

_____

2. Was Max second?

_____

3. Was Judy fifth?

_____

4. Who was fourth?

_____

5. Who was sixth?

_____

6. Was Sid eighth?

_____

7. Who was third?

_____

8. Was Dana second?

_____

B. Make sentences.

     Today   **Yesterday**

1. <u>They are playing catch.</u>   <u>They were playing catch.</u>

2. _____   _____

3. _____   _____

4. _____   _____

C. Read and connect.

1. Kay's birthday is on May 13th. She went bowling on her birthday.

2. Greg's birthday is on July 16th. He went out to eat on his birthday.

3. Ken's birthday is on April 29th. He went horseback riding on his birthday.

4. Sally's birthday is on September 11th. She had a party on her birthday.

D. Match and connect.

When's your birthday?	It's September 14th.
What's the date today?	You're kidding!
That's my birthday, too.	It's on November 5th.

Let's Talk

A. Match the answers and write.

No, I'm not.
Yes, I am.
Not yet.

Are you ready to go?

B. Unscramble and write.

go? | Are | you | to | ready

staying | I'm | home | No, | today.

Why?

throat. | I | sore | have | Because | a

C. Write the answers.

a cold	a headache	an earache	a sore throat
a fever	a stomachache	a toothache	a cough

1. Why did he stay home?

Because he had _____

2. Why did she stay home?

_____

3. Why did she stay home?

_____

4. Why did he stay home?

_____

5. Did he have a toothache?

_____

6. Did she have an earache?

_____

7. Did she have a headache?

_____

8. Did he have a sore throat?

_____

Let's Learn

A. Fill in the blanks. Then do the puzzle.

Across

3. make → _made_

4. do → _____

7. talk → _____

8. listen → _____

9. write → _____

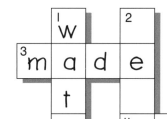

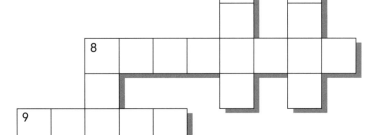

Down

1. watch → _watched_

2. read → _____

5. play → _____

6. stay → _____

8. look → _____

B. Write the answers.

1. What did he do in the morning?

_____

2. What did she do in the afternoon?

_____

3. What did he do in the evening?

_____

4. Did she write a letter in the morning?

_____

5. Did he play video games in the afternoon?

_____

6. Did she listen to music in the evening?

_____

C. What did you do last Saturday? Write the answers.

1. What did you do in the morning?

_____

2. What did you do in the afternoon?

_____

3. What did you do in the evening?

_____

Let's Read

A. Fill in the blanks.

| watched |
| took |
| was |
| called |
| ate |

Tracy's Diary

Saturday, April 20th

   Today _____ a boring day.

   I _____ TV all morning. Then

   I _____ my friend, Sandy.

She wasn't home. Then I _____

lunch and _____ a long nap.

B. Answer the questions.

1. What did Tracy do all morning?

_____

2. Did she call her friend?

_____

3. Did she play outside?

_____

Write your own question and answer.

4. _____

_____

C. Write in your diary.

_____

_____

_____

_____

_____

_____

_____

_____

D. Circle and write.

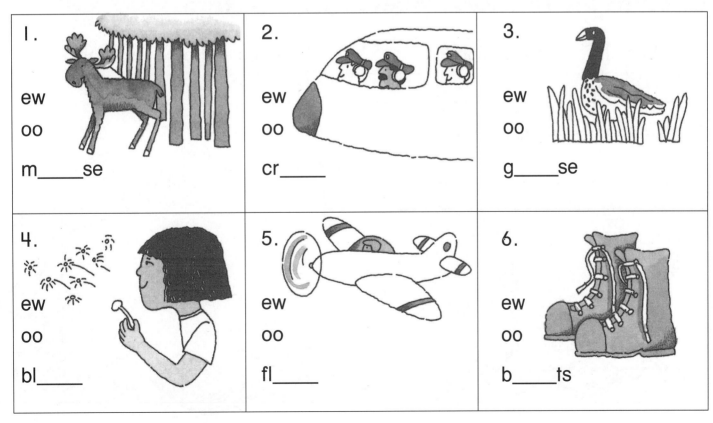

1.
ew
oo
m____se

2.
ew
oo
cr____

3.
ew
oo
g____se

4.
ew
oo
bl____

5.
ew
oo
fl____

6.
ew
oo
b____ts

Let's Sing

A. Unscramble and write the answers.

1. What did you do last night?

| fun | night. | last | had | I |

_____

2. Where did you go last night?

| home | I | stayed | night. | last |

_____

3. What did you do at home last night?

| last | did | I | home | homework |

| my | night. | at |

_____

B. Write the answers. Then draw a picture.

1. Did you have fun last night?

_____

2. Did you stay home last night?

_____

3. What did you do last night?

_____

A. Write the answers.

Hank   Marsha   Jon   Beth

1. Why did Jon stay at home?

_____

2. Why did Marsha stay at home?

_____

3. Why did Beth stay at home?

_____

4. Why did Hank stay at home?

_____

B. Write the answers.

1. What did she do?

_____

2. What did he do?

_____

3. What did they do?

_____

4. What did she do?

_____

Unit 6

Let's Talk

A. Fill in the blanks.

1. score	→	scored	2. get	→	_____
3. hit	→	_____	4. break	→	_____
5. catch	→	_____	6. _____	→	made
7. _____	→	won	8. happen	→	_____

B. Write the questions and the answers.

won a trophy   broke a window   won a race   scored a goal

1. <u>What happened?</u>

   <u>He won a race.</u>

2. _____

   _____

3. _____

   _____

4. _____

   _____

C. Write the answers.

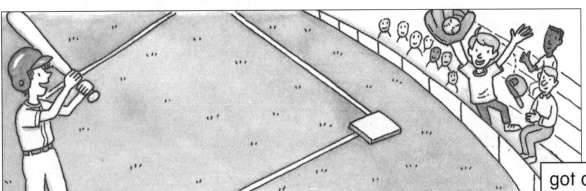

got an autograph
hit a home run
caught a ball
made a basket

1. What happened?

He _____

_____

He _____

_____

2. What happened?

She _____

_____

She _____

_____

Let's Learn

A. Write the words.

| down | over | into | around | under | out of |

1. _____over_____   2. _____   3. _____

4. _____   5. _____   6. _____

B. Look at the pictures. Then make sentences.

1. He	rode	into	a	pond.
2. She	walked	up	some	hill.
3. He	ran	through	a	woods.
4. She	walked	around	a	puddle.

C. Read and draw.

Bob went for a walk.
Where did he go?

He went through the woods.
He went around a pond.
He went under a bridge.
He went up a hill.
He went down the hill.
He went into a house.

D. Write your own story.

Sally went for a walk.
Where did she go?

She went _____

_____

_____

_____

_____

A. Fill in the blanks.

The Jets Win!

by Colleen Galloway

year
lost
exciting
won
tied
scored

The Jets had a very good _____. They _____ nine games and _____ one. They _____ one game. The last game was very _____. The Jets and the Bears were _____ two to two. Then Bobby Mills _____ a goal and they _____ the game. The Jets are the new champions!

B. True or false? Check the answers.

1. The Jets had a good year.   ☐ True   ☐ False

2. They won nine games and lost two games.   ☐ True   ☐ False

3. The last game was exciting.   ☐ True   ☐ False

Write your own true or false sentence.

4. _____   ☐ True   ☐ False

C. Circle and write.

1. oi oy b____	2. oi oy R____	3. oi oy f____l
4. oi oy c____l	5. oi oy s____l	6. oi oy t____

D. Write and draw.

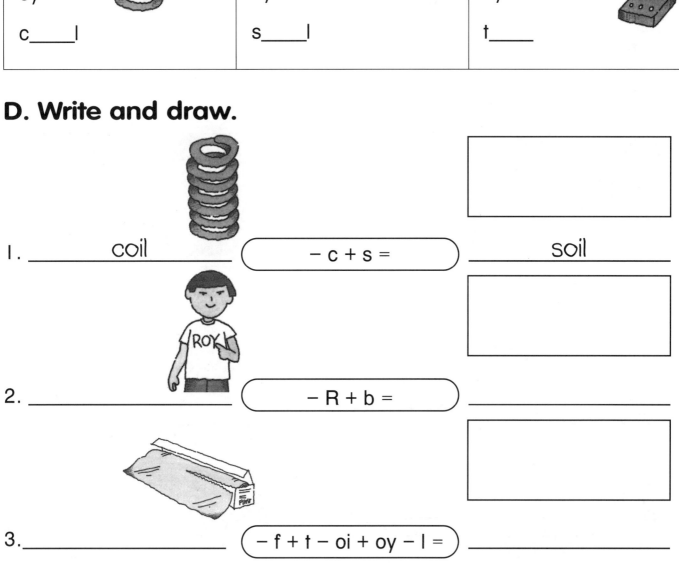

1. _____coil_____ (− c + s =) _____soil_____

2. _____ (− R + b =) _____

3. _____ (− f + t − oi + oy − l =) _____

Let's Chant

Write the questions and the answers.

1.

Guess what! _____
Guess what! He did it!

_____

What did he do?

_____

_____

_____

_____

3.

_____

_____

_____

_____

_____

4.

_____

_____

_____

_____

_____

A. Read and check the correct box.

☐   ☐

☐   ☐

1. The girl went for a run.
   She went into the woods.

2. The boys went for a bike ride.
   They went around some puddles.

B. What happened? Make sentences.

1. They _____

_____

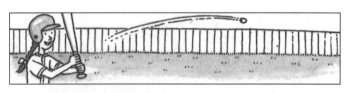

2. _____

_____

3. _____

_____

4. _____

_____

Let's Review

A. Write the answers.

1. Why did she stay home?

   Because she had _____

2. Why did he stay home?

   _____

3. Why did he stay home?

   _____

4. Why did she stay home?

   _____

B. Write the answers.

1. What did he do?

   _____

2. What did she do?

   _____

3. What did he do?

   _____

4. What did they do?

   _____

C. Write the answers.

1. What happened?

_____

2. What happened?

_____

3. Did she win a trophy?

_____

4. Did they win a race?

_____

D. Make sentences.

1. He went down a hill and around a pond.

2. _____

3. _____

4. _____

Let's Talk

A. Write the answers.

collect stamps	play tennis	go camping
play volleyball	go shopping	look at the stars

1. What does he like to do?

   He likes to _____

2. What does she like to do?

   _____

3. What do they like to do?

   _____

4. What does she like to do?

   _____

5. What does he like to do?

   _____

6. What do they like to do?

   _____

B. Write and draw.

What do you like to do?

_____

_____

_____

C. Change the sentences.

1. I like to go swimming.

   He <u>likes to go swimming.</u>

2. Pat doesn't like to roller-skate.

   I <u>don't like to roller-skate.</u>

3. She likes to go swimming.

   They _____

4. Tom likes to collect stamps.

   Sherri _____

5. They don't like to play tennis.

   Bob _____

6. Pam likes to go bike riding.

   We _____

7. Mike doesn't like to go shopping.

   They _____

8. Dave likes to play volleyball.

   Meg and Sue _____

9. They like to paint.

   He _____

10. Bob and Greg don't like to listen to music.

    I _____

Let's Learn

A. Write the answers.

| clear the table | sweep the floor | vacuum the carpet | dry the dishes |

1. What does he have to do?

He has to _____

2. What does she have to do?

_____

3. What do they have to do?

_____

4. What does he have to do?

_____

B. Complete the sentences.

| take out the trash | wash the dishes | feed the dog | set the table |

1. Bob wants to play outside,

but first he has to _____

_____

_____

2. Carol wants to read,

_____

_____

3. Sue and Chuck want to
   listen to music,

_____

_____

4. Nick wants to do a puzzle,

_____

_____

_____

C. Write the questions.

1. <u>Does he have to dry</u>
   <u>the dishes?</u>
   Yes, he does.

2. _____
   _____
   Yes, she does.

3. _____
   _____
   Yes, he does.

4. _____
   _____
   Yes, they do.

D. Check your answers.

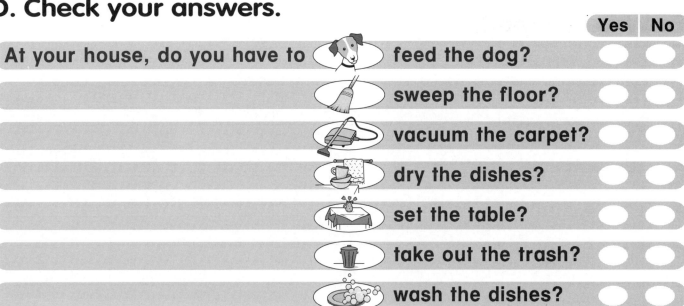

	Yes	No
At your house, do you have to feed the dog?	○	○
sweep the floor?	○	○
vacuum the carpet?	○	○
dry the dishes?	○	○
set the table?	○	○
take out the trash?	○	○
wash the dishes?	○	○

A. Fill in the blanks.

clear the table
get ready for bed
evening
set the table
wash the dishes
do his homework

John's Responsibilities

Every _____ John has a lot

to do. First he has to _____.

After dinner he has to _____

and _____. Then he

has to _____ Finally

he has to _____.

B. Write a report.

C. Circle and write.

1.

ow
ou

cl____d

2.

ow
ou

cl____n

3.

ow
ou

____l

4.

ow
ou

c____

5.

ow
ou

h____se

6.

ow
ou

m____se

D. Unscramble and draw.

1. l o w   o e h s u

   An _____ was flying

   over the _____

2. s e o u m   u d l c o

   The _____ was

   looking at the _____

E. Make a sentence using two of these words. Draw.

clown, owl, cow, cloud, house, mouse

_____

Let's Chant

A. Number the sentences. Then say the chant.

Oh no, I can't go bowling.

Don't worry, I can help you. I can teach you how.

1

Come on, let's go! Let's go bowling. Let's go bowling now.

I don't know how.

Why?

Come on, let's go! Let's go bowling. Let's go bowling now.

B. Answer the questions.

1. Do you know how to roller-skate?

2. Do you know how to swim?

_____

_____

Let's Listen

A. Complete the sentences.

| likes to | like to | has to | have to |

1. He _____
   look at the stars.

2. She _____
   clean up her room.

3. They _____
   go camping.

4. He _____
   do his homework.

5. They _____
   take out the trash.

6. She _____
   read books.

B. Write the answers.

1. Do you like to do your homework?

_____

2. Do you have to do your homework?

_____

Let's Talk

A. Write the questions and answers.

| a doctor | a movie star | a firefighter |
| a news reporter | a scientist | a photographer |

1. What does he want to be?

   He wants to be

2. _____

_____

3. _____

_____

4. _____

_____

5. _____

_____

6. _____

_____

B. Write and draw.

What do you want to be?

_____

_____

C. Write the questions and answers.

climb a mountain	fly an airplane	sail a boat	build a house

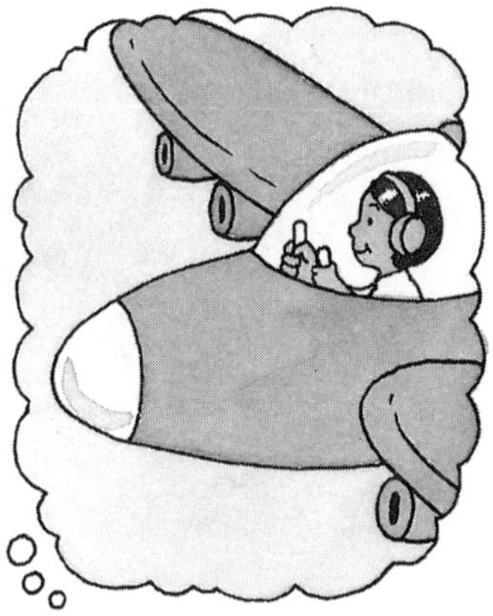

1. What does he want to do? _____

   He wants to _____

2. _____

   _____

3. _____

   _____

4. _____

   _____

D. Write and draw.

What do you want to do?

_____

_____

Let's Learn

A. Write the answers.

Frank   Marianne   Andrew   Sonya   Julie

1. What is Andrew going to do after school?

   He is going to _____

2. What is Marianne going to do after school?

   _____

3. What are Julie and Sonya going to do after school?

   _____

4. What is Frank going to do after school?

   _____

B. Answer the questions.

1. What are you going to do tomorrow morning?

   _____

2. What are you going to do tomorrow afternoon?

   _____

66

C. Change the words and complete the sentences.

1. Yesterday he played soccer.
   Tomorrow <u>he is going to</u> _____

   _____

2. Yesterday they played inside.
   Tomorrow _____

   _____

3. Yesterday they went swimming.
   Tomorrow _____

   _____

4. Yesterday she went to piano class.
   Tomorrow _____

   _____

D. Complete the sentences.

| 7:00 | 7:30 | 7:45 | 8:00 | 8:15 |

Now it is 7:00. Mike is waking up.

1. He <u>is going to school</u> at 8:15.
2. He _____ at 7:45.
3. He _____ at 8:00.
4. He _____ at 7:30.

Let's Read

A. Choose words from the boxes. Fill in the blanks.

My name is _____.
(1)

I'm in _____ grade.
(2)

I live in _____.
(3)

My father is _____.
(4)

I have _____.
(5)

I like to _____.
(6)

I want to be _____, too.
(7)

1
Mike
John
Sue
Jenny

2
third
fourth
fifth
sixth

3
Spain
Japan
Australia
America

4
an astronaut
a movie star
a news reporter
a photographer

5
a dog
a cat
a fish
a bird

6
listen to music
watch TV
play sports
collect stamps

7
an astronaut
a movie star
a news reporter
a photographer

B. Write about yourself. Follow the model on page 68.

C. Circle and write.

1.  au aw h___k	2.  au aw s___ce	3.  au aw n___ghty
4.  au aw f___n	5.  au aw l___n	6.  au aw ___tomobile

D. Write and draw.

_____ $- l + f =$ _____ $- f + h - n + k =$ _____

Let's Chant

Write the answers.

What do you want to be?

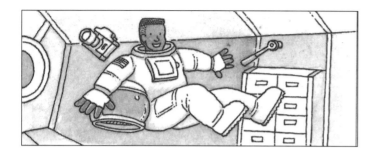 

1. <u>I want to be</u>   2. _____

3. _____ 4. _____

5. _____ 6. _____

7. _____ 8. _____

A. Unscramble and write the answers.

1. What does she want to be?

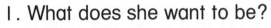
She wants to _____

2. What does he want to be?

_____

3. What does she want to do?

_____

4. What does she want to do?

_____

B. Answer the questions.

1. Is he going to talk on the telephone? No, he isn't. He is going to _____

_____

2. Is she going to study English? _____

_____

Let's Review

A. Answer the questions.

	Pete	Anne	Liza	Mary	Matt	Phil
play volleyball	✔	✔			✔	
go swimming			✔	✔		✔
use the computer	✔			✔	✔	
go bike riding		✔	✔			✔

1. Does Pete like to play volleyball?

   <u>Yes, he does. He likes to</u>
   <u>use the computer, too.</u>

2. Does Mary like to go bike riding?

   <u>No, she doesn't. She likes</u>
   <u>to go swimming and use</u>
   <u>the computer.</u>

3. Does Liza like to go swimming?

4. Does Anne like to use the computer?

5. Does Phil like to play volleyball?

6. Does Matt like to use the computer?

B. Make sentences.

What do you have to do?

1. <u>I have to wash the dishes.</u>

2. _____

3. _____

4. _____

C. Write the questions and the answers.

1. What does he want to do?
   He wants to climb a
   mountain.

2. What does she want to be?
   She wants to be an
   astronaut.

3. _____

   _____

4. _____

   _____

D. Make sentences.

Monday	Tuesday	Wednesday	Thursday	Friday	Saturday	Sunday
go swimming	go horseback riding	play baseball	go hiking	play volleyball	do arts and crafts	go home

The boys are at camp. Today is Thursday. They are hiking.

1. On Saturday <u>they are going to do arts and crafts.</u>

2. On Tuesday <u>they went horseback riding.</u>

3. On Friday _____

4. On Monday _____

5. On Wednesday _____

6. On Sunday _____

Complete the sentences and draw the pictures.

My House

My name is _____

My address is _____

My telephone number is _____

Draw a picture of your house.

My Friends

These are the addresses and telephone numbers of my friends.

Name ---
Address --
Telephone Number ---------------------------------------

Name ---
Address --
Telephone Number ---------------------------------------

Name ---
Address --
Telephone Number ---------------------------------------

Name ---
Address --
Telephone Number ---------------------------------------

Name ---
Address --
Telephone Number ---------------------------------------

Name ---
Address --
Telephone Number ---------------------------------------

Fill in the cards for six friends.

More Review

My Classroom

The name of my school is _____

I'm in _____ grade.

My teacher's name is _____

There are _____ boys and _____ girls in my class.

Draw a picture of your classroom.

More Review

My English Class

My English teacher's name is _____

There are _____ children in my English class.

In my English class I like to _____

Draw a picture of your English class.

My Calender

This month is _____. Today's date is _____.

Fill in the calendar for this month.
Write the month and the days of the week.
Then fill in the numbers.

My Birthday

My birthday is on _____

I'm _____ years old.

On my birthday I got _____

Draw your birthday present.

Birthdays in My Family

Name   **Birthday**

_____   _____

_____   _____

_____   _____

_____   _____

_____   _____

Fill in the names and birthdays of the people in your family.

Jobs

What does your father do?

My father is a _____

_____

What does your mother do?

My mother is a _____

_____

Draw a picture of your mother and father.

What do you want to be?

I want to _____

Draw a picture of yourself.

More Review